MW00435833

C-Change

How to Transform Any Business
Through the 7 Simple Principles
of Corporate Chaplaincy

The Transformation Series

Mark Cress

Author of Bestselling Novel *The Third Awakening*

C-Change: How to Transform Any Business Through the 7 Simple Principles of Corporate Chaplaincy
By Mark Cress
Copyright ©2005 Mark Cress

ISBN 0-9762151-4-4
For Worldwide Distribution
Printed in the U.S.A.

Lanphier Press
U.S.A.
www.lanphierpress.com

Table of Contents

❦ Dedication

Every day, all over America, corporate chaplains are caring for hundreds of thousands of employees who are experiencing countless tragedies and difficulties. Those chaplains are my true heroes, and I dedicate this book to them.

🦋 Preface

The question is frequently asked, "How long has corporate chaplaincy really been in existence?" The most accurate answer is most likely, "As long as there has been commerce."

In Old Testament times, godly people in the marketplace likely had the same ministry goal as those in Jesus' time and in our time. The answer to what they had in common is simple. True corporate chaplains are constantly building relationships with people in the workplace, in order to gain the right to care for them in God's Name whenever a crisis erupts in their lives. Because we live in a fallen world that lacks any resemblance to perfection, almost everyone in the workplace is either just coming out of, in the middle of, or about to enter some kind of personal or business crisis.

Learning the "7 C's" of corporate chaplaincy will open new vistas of leadership and caring for individuals. Implementing them in the life of a business will transform it for future success and eternally impact the lives of its employees in the process.

As you read this little book, whether you are in the executive suite or are laboring at an entry level job, consider asking God to use these principles to transform you for greater joy and fulfillment in one of the greatest mission fields on earth...the marketplace.

❦ Acknowledgements

A book like this finds its way to print only after many hours of dedication from people other than the author. My job is actually the easiest. I start every writing session by asking God to give me the thoughts, and the words, to simply tell a story. The hard part then comes for a delightful group of people who are imminently more talented than I.

Once I finish a chapter, I call on a group that has affectionately become known as "The Rough Reader Gang." They read my rough text and make recommendations for changes that will enhance the overall work. These hardy souls are Randy Clark, Jeff Hilles, Chris Hobgood, Ellen McNally, Dwayne Reece, Frank Reed, and Cindy Rice. My precious wife Linda and "baby girl" Avery also read everything I write and offer encouragement that keeps me at the keys.

Once my administrative assistant, Cindy Rice, corrects all of my bad grammar and the words I have tricked my computer into misspelling, she sends the manuscript for its final level of editing by Robin Crabtree and Mike Wolff. Throughout the process Robin works on the design and with the publisher and printer on pre-press issues. Jess Duboy advises on readability and offers tremendous expertise in many other areas. Thanks to José Rondón for textual advice. Howard Piekarz and the fine staff at Edwards Brothers really hustled to bring this book to press with lightning speed and great efficiency. I offer my heartfelt thanks and appreciation to all.

— *Mark Cress*, Summer 2005

🦋 Introduction

Over the last decade I have had the great fortune to serve God through the mission of Corporate Chaplains of America. In the earliest days I was the ministry's first chaplain and founder. I am now blessed to guide the national organization as its President and CEO.

My calling and heart, however, is still that of a corporate chaplain. I continue to serve in that role at the first two companies that signed on with our organization, Price's Auto Parts and Price's Paint and Body. Since the beginning days of our work, God has allowed me to serve many people who have endured extraordinarily difficult situations. As a chaplain, I have worked with employees who have faced every type of problem described in the pages of this book. Even though I have permission to tell their stories, each account has been modified somewhat, in order to protect the identities of both the companies and the individuals.

Each chapter begins with a story in the life of an imaginary new chaplain, serving in a fictitious company. Although each of these stories is real, they did not occur over a four month period as portrayed in the book. It would not, however, be impossible for that to occur.

CHAPTER ONE

Transforming Principle Number One

"CHRIST"

Lonnie had been dreaming of this day for the past year, ever since he first heard the term "corporate chaplain" at a workplace ministry retreat at church. It was as if God spoke directly to his heart and said, "All your time in the workplace, all the hard hours of study in seminary, and every hour you have spent in church ministry over the past five years were all leading up to My calling you to serve Me in the workplace." The thought was so clear in his mind that Lonnie knew it had to be from God, and yet the idea of becoming a chaplain was new to him.

Nevertheless, things seemed to be happening very quickly. The transition had been smooth so far, but now he wasn't so sure of his decision. After going through many interviews and training classes, leaving his loving congregation and moving his family halfway across the country, he now found his heart racing. Lonnie began to wonder if he might even be experiencing a heart attack. He felt like a kid fresh out of college facing his first day on a new job, sitting here in his car in the parking lot of Reynolds Industries. Lonnie was about to enter Reynolds alone for the first time as the company's new corporate chaplain.

Only last week he had been here with his ministry supervisor for a day of orientation meetings with all the employees. They came to the lunch room in groups of twenty or thirty and heard his boss, Mike Hilles, explain how the program worked and how he, Lonnie Pepper, was going to be their chaplain. He was relieved that they would just know him as Lonnie, like a friend, instead of Reverend Pepper. He had often chuckled inwardly when the people at the church referred to him as Dr. Pepper. Over the years it had been both funny and at times a little annoying. Sometimes he even wondered why he pursued the Doctor of Ministry Degree from the seminary in the first place. But now he could finally just be Lonnie, the company chaplain: A friend who would be there no matter what kind of crisis came their way. A friend who didn't have to chair committees, attend deacon meetings, prepare and deliver the weekly sermon, or help select the color of the carpet for the sanctuary. No, just Lonnie the caregiver, in the strangest of all mission fields,

a seat belt factory. A place where seventy percent of the workers had stopped going to church a long time ago, if they had ever attended in the first place. A place where

A friend who would be there no matter what kind of crisis came their way.

people spent most of their waking hours and where employees carried their problems from home straight through the front door with them each morning. He reminded himself that this was not just a seat belt factory; no, it was a lot more than that. Like every other business in America, and even around the world, it was a place where relationships were built. Sometimes these relationships were for the best and sometimes they were not. It was a place where people were more transparent than the folks he was used to ministering to every week at the church. He knew that most of the time people came to church trying to look and act as if their lives were perfect, all the while hiding behind a wall of family secrets. This had always been a source of frustration for him.

But sitting in the car at this very moment, he almost found himself wishing he were back in his comfortable office at the church. His stomach was full of butterflies. Why would Lonnie Pepper be nervous? He had stood before hundreds every week delivering sermons. Only a few weeks ago he had been considered one of the pillars of the community. He was on the board of the community hospital and had served as president of the local Rotary club. Everyone knew Reverend Pepper. Why would the thought of getting out of the car and walking into this factory seem so daunting all of a sudden?

Average, ordinary people were streaming past him and heading into the building as naturally as the rising of the sun. Yet here he sat, his hands shaking, his heart racing, and every instinct in his body telling him to flee. "Just start the engine and get out of here as fast as you can!" Why was the thought of going into this company such a challenge? It was as if he was heading into the deepest part of the jungle and the natives might eat him for dinner. Whatever it was, Lonnie was unaccustomed to being so nervous prior to a ministry opportunity. He was fastened to his seat as tightly as if a team of Reynold's finest employees had specially fitted his car with a seat belt designed to prohibit him from exiting the vehicle.

He told himself to get a grip as he reached for his Palm Pilot in order to look up a Bible verse that might give him comfort. After reading a few verses from the Psalms, he began to pray, asking God to give him peace. His mind drifted back to days he had just spent with the other new chaplains in training. He reflected on the words of Chris, the corporate trainer for the agency to which God had called him.

Chris was a very experienced chaplain. Prior to attending seminary he had had a successful career as a corporate trainer. Now God was making use of both sets of highly developed skills in his position as Associate Vice President for Chaplain Development. Lonnie had really bonded with Chris. He trusted him and knew the things he was learning about ministry in the workplace were not only valid, but also essential to his success in the field.

But it was all so different. Chris had told him that within the first ninety days or so of starting at Reyn-

...in time almost all of the employees would see him as part of their families.

olds he would attain an almost diplomatic status at the company, and in time almost all of the employees would see him as part of their families. They would share with him the most intimate problems in their lives and count on him for guidance and spiritual care. For now that seemed like a lifetime away. What had he missed? Why the anxiety? Was he losing his mind? Had he misinterpreted what he thought to be God's call on his life? He knew from a practical point of view that all he needed to do was get out of the car and walk through the back door of the company and begin greeting employees, learning their names and earning the right to build a relationship with them. Unfortunately, the practical side of his brain was quickly giving way to the emotional side, and he just wasn't sure he could do it.

After a few more minutes that seemed like hours,

he slowly pulled his cell phone from his side and dialed a local number. He was doing what came naturally in a situation like this. He was reaching out to his best friend, his wife Sandy. She answered after only one ring and said in her ever cheerful and familiar voice, "Hey there, Chaplain Dr. Pepper! Have you rescued anyone from the furnace yet today?" The levity of her precious voice helped calm Lonnie. She had always been there to encourage him, and now she was doing it again. Before he could tell her he was about to come home and call it quits without ever entering the building, she told him she had been praying for him all morning and had a sense in her heart that God was about to use him in a great way in his new mission field.

After a few more moments on the phone, he told her he loved her and pressed the end button and stared as her name vanished from the screen on the phone. He looked at his watch and realized he would soon need to be in the building, or he would miss an opportunity to mill around with the employees during the shift change. Suddenly the flood of emotions was back, and to add to the discomfort of the pangs in his stomach, he was now sweating profusely. For whatever reason, he decided to grab his training manual and look over the section dedicated to the early days of making rounds at a new company.

As he flipped from page to page, nothing seemed to jump out that would ease his emotional trauma. Nothing, that is, until he reached the final page of the section. The answer to his current anxiety hit him like a ton of bricks. Why hadn't he thought of this before? Chris had been so thorough on this point, and yet he was about to leave it out altogether. There it was in bold print:

Always say this prayer before getting out of your vehicle and entering any company: "God, I pray that the employees under my care today will see in me Christ Jesus, the hope of glory."

As he read those words, tears filled his eyes. He dropped his head and first asked God to forgive him, and then quietly and peacefully prayed the simple prayer. Suddenly, and miraculously, the burden was lifted. He felt peaceful and strong. He pulled the handle on the door, slipped from behind the wheel, closed the door behind him, pressed the lock button on his key fob, and strolled comfortably and confidently toward the building.

As he made his way into the large common area where many employees were gathering for the next shift, he smiled and began to exchange greetings, handshakes, and pats on the back. Before he knew it, he had made his way all around the plant. A couple of people had told him stories about their kids, a few wanted to know which NASCAR driver he liked or disliked. One even asked to talk with him at break time about a problem. Never again would he forget to say the simple prayer, and neither would he forget the essential nature and centrality of Christ in his ministry as a spiritual caregiver in the workplace.

Leadership Transformers From
Chapter One

- 🦋 **Change is stressful.** The best leaders embrace it like a best friend.

- 🦋 **People hate surprises.** Use effective orientation procedures with small groups of employees to introduce new concepts.

- 🦋 **Never fear people.** There is no record in American economic history where someone was cannibalized in the workplace.

- 🦋 **Watch for wisdom.** Always be ready to look back to times of training for a "nugget of wisdom" in a time of crisis.

- 🦋 **Ask for advice.** Don't be afraid to seek counsel from a trusted friend or associate when difficult situations arise.

- 🦋 **Procrastination breeds failure.** The toughest part of any assignment is getting started. Once you get any object in motion, it doesn't take as much energy to keep it moving forward.

🦋 **Focus on finishing.** Never confuse activity with accomplishment. Attending meetings and chairing committees should never be a substitute for rolling up your sleeves and making something happen.

Leader's Ultimate Transformer Take Away

Embrace change like a best friend and master ways to help others do the same thing.

C-Changer's Transforming Thought

"Know Christ, know leadership. No Christ, no leadership."

– Unknown

C-Change

Caregiving Transformers From Chapter One

🦋 **Trust God's plan.** Everything that has happened in your life up to this point has been part of God's plan to prepare you for the workplace ministry He has in store for you now.

🦋 **Open the door.** When God has something for you to do, He will make it known to you.

🦋 **Abandon your ego.** Leave your fancy titles at the door. Remember, the superstars are so great that people remember them by one name: Tiger, Michael, Oprah, Lance, and Jesus.

🦋 **Study the Word.** God can always use the Scriptures to speak to a heart about a stressful situation.

🦋 **Two become one.** Work hard at making your spouse the best friend you have in life and ministry.

🦋 **Let Christ shine.** Always pray that people will see in you Christ Jesus, the hope of glory, instead of simply you in all of your humanity.

🦋 **Bloom where planted.** Your mission field is where God has you planted right now, not some imaginary jungle you may never physically encounter.

Caregiver's Ultimate Transformer Take Away

Jesus Christ is the center of the universe and everything else revolves around Him. Without Him, none of the other "7 C's" matter at all. He is the glue that holds the entire world together, and without Him no genuine workplace ministry will occur.

Transformed by the Word

"In Christ Jesus, then, I have legitimate reason to glory in my work for God in what through Christ Jesus I have accomplished concerning the things of God."

– Romans 15:17 (Amplified Bible)

CHAPTER TWO

Transforming Principle Number Two

"CALL"

I t had now been two full weeks since that first clumsy morning when Lonnie began his rounds as a chaplain at Reynolds Industries. At training he was challenged, along with all the other trainees in the class, to strive to be able to recognize the majority of his employees by name within the first couple of months in the field. That might not have been so tough if he only cared for the 320 employees at Reynolds, but his new mission field included about 100 employees at a local trucking terminal, 90 employees at three small auto quick-lube locations, and 140 employees at a local beer distributor, of all places.

It was there that Lonnie received confirmation of his true calling to be a chaplain in the workplace, during his first Friday morning rounds visit. The HR director welcomed him and invited him to participate in the company's Red Cross blood drive. Lonnie, like all participants, would receive a twelve pack of beer for his donation of a pint of blood. The restrained chuckle Lonnie gave was only a slight indication of the humor he found in the offer. He found himself starkly confronted with the realization that he was not ministering to only the church any longer.

Yet, learn names he did, and his motivation to do so increased as he saw on the face of each employee how much it meant when he recognized them and treated them like a family member. As he moved through the plant on this particular morning, he found himself making mental notes of the people and issues he would encounter. There was Betty, whose mother was very ill in a nursing home in another state, and Barry, whose wife was battling cancer. A guy named Jimmy in shipping was separated from his wife and was open to Lonnie meeting with the two of them in an effort to start a reconciliation process. Then there was Susan, who had lost her husband in a tragic car crash only last month. All of a sudden it hit him that in only a couple of weeks, God had given to him the opportunity to care for people in ways he never had before. He stopped and thanked the Lord, and once again he lifted each of these precious people up in prayer.

Susan's case really hit home for Lonnie. Her husband's death and the way it occurred were all too familiar. Lonnie's best friend in seminary, Bill Perry, had been killed by a drunk driver only four months earlier. The incident seemed more tragic because Bill had been driving home from a Wednesday evening prayer service at his church in Dothan, Alabama. The hole that

Her husband's death and the way it occurred were all too familiar.

Bill's death left in Lonnie's heart still ached every day. He and Bill had remained very close since their seminary days. Generally they had e-mailed each other every day and talked on the phone at least once a week. Their families had vacationed together every year since they left school. Lonnie was very proud of Bill. He had been one of the brightest students in his seminary graduating class, and the church in Dothan was the largest pastored by any of the members of their class. Lonnie had spoken there for Bill several times in the past couple of years, and he was always impressed with how the church had grown under his dear friend's leadership. Why had God chosen to take him home so early in life and while such great ministry had been going on in the life of the church?

Bill's wife, Lora, and their three kids had decided to stay in Dothan and the church was doing a good job of ministering to their needs, but the grief process continued for everyone associated with the tragedy. Bill had encouraged Lonnie regarding corporate chaplaincy, even though the idea was a totally new concept to them both. Bill had even admitted to being caught a little off guard when Lonnie became serious about the prospect of leaving the church for a ministry in the workplace. During the last couple of weeks Lonnie often found himself thinking of Bill, wondering if he would approve and just wishing he could talk to him about what was going on.

One of the hardest things about making rounds at Reynolds was going through the fabrication plant. The supervisor in that department, Johnny, was not a very nice person. On his very first day of rounds through the area, Johnny made it very clear to Lonnie that he wanted nothing to do with the chaplain program or Lonnie in particular. He even used some fairly foul language to punctuate his point. He also made his feelings known to others under his supervision, which threw a cold blanket on Lonnie's ability to engage the rest of the group. What made it all the more difficult was that, even though they were polar opposite personalities, Johnny could have been an exact double for Lonnie's old seminary friend, Bill. It was uncanny, almost as if they had been identical twins separated from their mother at birth. These two issues really made Lonnie dread going into the Fab Shop.

Ironically, however, the first part of the problem fit exactly into a pattern he had learned about in training. He had been told that the employees' initial opinions about the chaplain program would basically form a standard bell curve. About ten percent would immediately think that adding a chaplain program at the company was the greatest thing in the world and would happily embrace the program and the chaplain. The middle eighty percent would essentially be neutral and have the opinion that the program might help others in the company with problems, but they would most likely never need the services of the chaplain. Johnny fell into the latter ten percent. These are the people who generally don't like any program the company initiates, and for the most part are suffering with personal issues that make it difficult to get along with anyone.

Lonnie had been well trained by Chris on how to work in this environment. He was impressed with how the agency he was now serving used this data to build a training model for the chaplains in the field. When used effectively, the model would consistently change

Lonnie had been well trained by Chris on how to work in this environment.

the shape of the bell curve, making it possible to have a sincere ministry with the overwhelming majority of the employees within the first 180 days of service to a company.

He knew, however, that this training would truly be put to the test with Johnny and the people in his department. He was also having trouble coping with his own emotions in dealing with Johnny, as it related to his own grieving process.

"CALL"

While finishing his rounds for the day at Reynolds, Lonnie felt the familiar *chirp, vibrate* of his pager. It took a brief moment for him to realize that the unfamiliar set of digits was his own home phone number. He was still adjusting to the new area code and was shocked that he had not yet fully memorized his own number.

As he exited the plant, Lonnie immediately called his wife, Sandy. She wanted to know what time he would be coming home. Showing a bit of concern, he immediately asked if everything was alright. "Are the kids okay? What's going on?" She quickly calmed his nerves and told him that she was just wondering if he would be coming home for lunch. A letter had arrived for him, but it didn't seem to be urgent.

Before he could ask whom the letter was from, his pager sounded again. Lonnie recognized the, by now, familiar number of the Human Resources director at Reynolds Industries. Without thinking any further about the letter, he told Sandy he planned to be home for lunch but needed to make a quick call and would be there soon. He called the HR manager, Jill, as soon as he hung up with Sandy. Jill was just calling to let him

29

know of an e-mail she had received from Betty, one of the Reynolds' employees. Betty wanted the leadership of Reynolds to know how much she appreciated the chaplain's care and concern for her mother, and how much it meant to her when Lonnie arranged for a fellow corporate chaplain from her mother's area to visit her in the nursing home. "It's great to get encouraging feedback so soon," Lonnie thought as he put the cell phone back in the pouch and headed home for lunch.

As he walked in the door of his new home, Lonnie thought about how nice it was to be able to dash in for lunch before making afternoon rounds at the lube shops. Sandy greeted him with a big hug, as the aroma of her special tuna salad sandwiches filled the air. She handed him the letter with a puzzled look in her eyes as he read the return address: Celebration Christian Fellowship, Dothan, Alabama. The letter was brief and to the point:

Dear Reverend Pepper:

After much prayer, review of your past ministry service and receiving unanimous positive input from members of our church family, the Elders of Celebration Christian Fellowship would like to invite you and your family to consider meeting with our committee in view of a possible call to serve as our Senior Pastor. We realize you have just recently moved to a new city to serve as a chaplain, but hope you will consider seriously our invitation to return to a position of genuine, meaningful local church ministry. Our chairman Aldis Harrington, MD will be calling you in the next few days to discuss how we have come to the conclusion that you are the best person for our position.

Respectfully,
Committee of Elders
Celebration Fellowship

As he stared at the words on the page, it was as if he had just been hit in the stomach with a fast-ball that had knocked the wind completely out of his system. Rubbing his left hand through his hair, his right hand that was holding the letter dropped by his side. He looked over to see the expression on Sandy's face, gazing at her in disbelief. Various disconnected thoughts flashed through his head, "What is God up to here? We just finished moving in! Dothan is eight hours closer to our folks than where we are standing right now! The people at these companies are counting on me! Why is this church sending this letter to me at this time? Celebration is a great place with a terrific future. Do I need to do this to honor Bill? I was convinced God was calling us here!"

The freight train of thoughts kept swirling in his head. Sandy could sense what he was going through by the look on his face, even though there was complete silence in the room. She looked up and placed her index finger on her lips as if to quiet his thoughts. Oddly, this gesture brought him back to the present. She then put her arms around him and drew him close. Sandy uncharacteristically began to pray aloud. This was strange only because it was Lonnie who always led their prayer times together each day. Without realizing it, she began asking God questions in her prayers. To her amazement, she found herself quoting Bible verses back to Him in the prayer that seemed to answer each question. The verses she was involuntarily quoting were the very same ones Lonnie had used several months before to encourage her that God was calling them to serve in the workplace. Yet, she had never really committed them to memory.

After what seemed to be an eternity of hugging and semi-conscious praying, the session ended. They looked into each other's eyes and, for whatever reason, began to laugh. As the laughter continued, the feeling of relief began to build. Within a few minutes, they were hugging again. This time it was Lonnie who was talking to God, thanking Him for truly calling him into His service as a corporate chaplain. Lonnie knew for certain he was squarely in the center of God's will for his life.

Leadership Transformers From Chapter Two

🦋 **Leaders learn names.** They use them often in active conversation.

🦋 **Visit your people.** Managing by walking around is as important today as at any time in business history.

🦋 **Always be sensitive.** Be especially aware of the personal issues facing your subordinates.

🦋 **Master your mission.** There will always be employees who do not understand your mission and will try to undermine your authority. Be patient and formulate a plan to bring them around.

🦋 **Trust the curve.** Remember the "10-80-10 Bell Curve Rule" in managing people. Ten percent of your employees will readily follow your leadership; eighty percent have a herd mentality and are followers; and ten percent don't follow anyone, think any idea you have is crazy, and don't even like their own mothers.

🦋 **Cultivate company call.** Innovate employee retention systems that allow employees to feel "called" to serve your company for the long term.

🦋 **Lock your call.** Make sure you have locked down the matter of feeling "called" to your leadership position.

Leader's Ultimate Transformer Take Away

Always remember that people are individuals. They will not all think like you or respond equally to the same kind of management techniques. Leaders learn the art of connecting with many different personality types without losing their own personal bearing.

C-Changer's Transforming Thought

"I believe the will of God prevails; without Him all human reliance is vain; without the assistance of that Divine Being I cannot succeed; with that assistance I cannot fail."
– Abraham Lincoln

Caregiving Transformers from Chapter Two

🦋 **Know your people.** One of the quickest ways to gain the respect of people for whom you are caring is to recognize them by name.

🦋 **Crises are real.** Almost everyone in your workplace mission field is either just coming out of a crisis, in the middle of a crisis, or about to enter some form of crisis.

🦋 **Evil does exist.** Because we live in a fallen world, bad things happen to decent, hard-working people.

🦋 **Keep conversations private.** Never discuss an employee's personal problem or health issue in a manner that will allow other people to hear your conversation.

🦋 **Expect spiritual warfare.** Never expect Satan to fight fair.

🦋 **Run from distractions.** Keep firmly in mind what God has called you to do, so you will not be distracted by every wind that blows in the form of a new ministry opportunity.

🦋 **Call on God.** Whenever you are confused, call on God for clarity.

Caregiver's Ultimate Transformer Take Away

When God has called you to do something, He will make sure that you have every asset necessary to accomplish the task and will stick by you to its conclusion. Always resist abandoning Him along the way.

Transformed by the Word

"The LORD says, 'I will guide you along the best pathway for your life. I will advise you and watch over you.'"

– Psalms 32:8 (NLT)

CHAPTER THREE

Transforming Principle Number Three

"CONFIDENTIALITY"

Although it had only been a couple of weeks since Lonnie had sent a grateful, yet declining, letter of response to Celebration Church, it seemed like more than a year had passed. He had begun to get into a good flow with making rounds, and more and more people were beginning to open up about issues in their lives and circumstances from their past. Hearing the stories of grief, loss, betrayal, remorse, fear, and anger always made him realize what a sheltered life he and Sandy had been living over the past fifteen years. It also reinforced what a wonderful job his own parents had done in raising his sister, brother, and him. Lonnie had studied family of origin issues in Dr. Carlisle's counseling classes in seminary, but the issues always seemed so distant. That certainly was not the case anymore; he was now coming face to face with them nearly every day. He often found himself wishing he had paid a little better attention during those sessions.

Lonnie's prayer list of employee needs was growing by the day. Just looking at the list every morning reinforced what a great need there was for chaplaincy in the workplace and just how much God was already using him in the lives of ordinary people who sometimes found themselves facing extraordinarily difficult circumstances in life. The diversity of people with whom he came in contact every day made his ministry less monotonous than he once feared it might become.

Chris had told Lonnie and the other chaplain trainees that the very best workplace caregivers quickly developed the ability to spend at least four times as much time listening than talking when it came to caring for employees. With each new day he was finding this to be very good advice. "Strategic listening", as it was called, was almost becoming a game in which Lonnie competed against himself, always looking to improve his technique. He found himself reflecting on his encounters with employees who would engage him in conversation about needs in their lives. Lonnie clearly saw that the four to one ratio of listening to talking had a powerful impact on just how deeply the person would open up to him. Chris had also told him it wouldn't take long for an employee or two who were particularly hurting to really open up and seek his help. This could not have been more true as it related to the swirling vortex of complexity in the life of a semi-skilled worker named Manuel. Just after orientation, Manuel had started opening up to Lonnie about some minor issues in his life. Little did Lonnie know how the level and intensity of the issues were about to change.

During these early conversations, Manuel was only testing the waters with Lonnie to see if he could really talk to him about the major problems his family was facing. Lonnie found himself at the company about thirty minutes before the start of the workday on his fourth Friday of rounds at Reynolds. As Lonnie was getting out of his car, Manuel spoke to him through the open window of the car parked next to his and asked if he would sit and talk for a minute.

Lonnie opened the door and slid into the front seat next to Manuel. Their initial conversation started out like many do between workplace chaplains and employees facing tragically difficult problems. Manuel asked the question that Lonnie had now been asked in different ways a few times on rounds at his various companies, "Are you sure you won't tell anyone what I say to you?" It was as if a pool of tears was dammed up behind the sad eyes that stared deeply at Lonnie that morning. Manuel finally decided to fully open up about the problems he was facing. Lonnie gave assurances of his confidentiality pledge, yet later he would admit to the Lord in his prayers how unprepared he had been for the story that followed.

Manuel started by telling Lonnie about his family, his wife of twelve years, Madie, and their three kids, Juan, who was eleven, eight-year-old Tony and one-year-old Maggie. He told Lonnie about his love for his family and how they had moved from New York about a year ago just after Maggie was born. He was born in Puerto Rico and moved to New York with his parents when he was little. He and Madie had enjoyed a wonderful life together until last year, when calamity struck at the strangest of all places, a hospital in New York City.

Madie had fallen when she was eight months pregnant with Maggie. Something happened internally that caused her to hemorrhage. She lost a lot of blood and needed a transfusion. Because of faulty testing she was given HIV infected blood. Eventually Madie and little Maggie tested HIV positive. Their extended family and close friends reacted very differently than they expected, mostly fearing the spread of the virus. Within weeks of the diagnosis, they found themselves isolated from friends and family and decided to leave for a town where no one would know.

Because of faulty testing she was given HIV infected blood.

Manuel loved working at Reynolds. He was a model employee and had quickly made friends with the guys on his shift. However, both Madie and Maggie were now symptomatic for full-blown AIDS. Manuel and his family feared that as soon as people at Reynolds found out, they would be shunned once again, but this time in a strange city. All he wanted Lonnie to do was pray for God to heal his wife and little girl.

Lonnie did pray for Manuel and his family. He also reassured him that he would continue to pray and would be there for them no matter what. It was the "no matter what" that Lonnie had no idea would be required so soon after their brief meeting in the car that pleasant spring morning. Manuel ended their meeting with almost the same question with which he started, "Can I really trust you to keep this to yourself?" Lonnie reassured him, and they both made their way into the plant. Lonnie's heart was broken for Manuel and his family. He was certain if the owners of the company knew what this family was going through, they would help in every way possible, but he was bound not to share a word with anyone. As he made his rounds, his mind kept going back to the brief meeting with Manuel in the little Nissan.

Lonnie had stopped by the hospital to check on an employee who recently had a baby when his pager went off. This time it was the safety manager at Reynolds, Joe Stein. He informed Lonnie that there had been an accident involving one of the company trucks. Manuel Regis, the driver, was a little shaken emotionally but no one was hurt. Joe was wondering if Lonnie might swing by the plant and check on Manuel when he returned from the standard "critical incident drug test" later in the day. Lonnie asked Joe to page him again when Manuel was back at the plant, and he would come right over.

When his pager went off later in the day to the same number, he almost drove directly to the plant. Instead he decided to call Joe and let him know he was on the way. When Joe answered the phone, it was obvious that he was shaken up. He told Lonnie to call the HR department regarding Manuel. When Lonnie reached Jill in HR, she told him that they were all shocked. Manuel's drug test had come back positive. Unfortunately according to company policy, he would be terminated by the end of the workday. Lonnie was momentarily speechless. Thoughts spiraled through his mind, and at first he didn't quite know what to do. Jill asked Lonnie if he could be available at the company following the termination, in case Manuel wanted to speak with the chaplain. She had no way of knowing the thoughts that were going through Lonnie's mind at that exact moment. He said he would be there, and they ended their conversation.

Lonnie hung up the phone, pulled to the side of the road and began to pray. He made a mental note not to make a habit of returning pages from his mobile phone while driving the car. He was surprised and thankful he didn't have a wreck himself when Jill gave him the news. He went on to pray for Manuel and also for Jill and the other managers who were facing such a difficult afternoon.

Lonnie hung up the phone, pulled to the side of the road and began to pray.

Following the time of prayer, he called his ministry supervisor and without giving any names or a company name, briefly laid out the situation and asked for advice. Although he had never had a case like this before, his supervisor was a seasoned chaplain who had been through many tough cases in the field. He gave Lonnie a few pointers, and then offered a prayer for the entire situation. Within a few minutes, Lonnie was back underway and nearing the plant. His mind was swirling. He wished he could call Sandy and tell her all of this, but he knew he couldn't. The best he could do was let her know that he might be late for dinner because he was working on a case and to ask her to pray for the situation with which he was involved.

When he arrived at the plant he stopped by Jill's office. He remembered that during his training Chris had emphasized the importance of gaining permission before acting. While he was careful not to breach the trust Manuel had placed in him, he was hoping that he could get Jill to understand the relationship he had developed with Manuel during their brief session. This might allow him to break the news in a more personal manner. Lonnie asked Jill's permission to talk with Manuel prior to the termination meeting. Having never been faced with a situation like this with the chaplain before, she didn't quite know how to answer his request. She knew she had to be careful to protect the company regarding the legalities of human resource management, but there was nothing in her manuals or from her training that covered a situation like this. Reluctantly she gave permission, but warned that the policy was the policy and the consequences were not likely to change.

Lonnie went to the place in the plant where he was

most apt to find Manuel, and thankfully he was there. He smiled when he looked up and saw Lonnie and immediately asked if Lonnie knew about the accident. Lonnie asked him if they could once again sit in the car for a little talk. As they sat there, Lonnie wasn't really sure where to start. He began by asking Manuel about the accident, and then inquired if Manuel knew the results of the drug test. With a puzzled look, Manuel asked if there was a problem. Lonnie lowered his head and told Manuel he had tested positive for marijuana. He went on to tell him he had the right to be retested, and that the company was planning to let him go at the end of the day.

Tears streamed down Manuel's face. He said a second test wouldn't be necessary. He then told Lonnie about the visits he and Madie had with the doctor about the extreme pain Madie was experiencing. They couldn't afford the pain medication the doctor had prescribed, because the company medical plan didn't cover it. The doctor said he couldn't prescribe or professionally condone smoking pot, but that it would certainly ease Madie's pain, although not as effectively as the medication would have. She and Manuel had never smoked pot before, but he hated watching her suffer. One day he broke down and bought the pot from a guy in their neighborhood he didn't even know. For the past couple of weeks, each night after the kids were all in bed asleep, he and Madie would lock the door to their bedroom and she would smoke the drug to relieve the pain. Because the room was small and they sealed the bottom of the door with a towel to protect the children, Manuel was inhaling the smoke as he sat beside Madie on the bed.

When words suddenly failed, he looked at Lonnie and broke down in tears. Lonnie found himself crying as he began to pray for God to intervene. Thinking back to his conversation with his ministry supervisor, he asked Manuel if he could have permission to speak with the company owner, David Reynolds, about the entire situation in an effort to save Manuel's job and possibly get some help for his family. Manuel said he had never known a company owner who would care about such matters. Lonnie assured him that Mr. Reynolds was a wonderful Christian man. Even though he couldn't offer any assurances, things were so bleak that they had little left to lose and time was certainly working against them at this point. Manuel dropped his head as his shoulders drooped. All he could think about was the devastation of having to go home and

He looked up at Lonnie and apologized for dragging him into the situation.

tell Madie he was out of work with no hope of finding a job to support their family. His chest was tight, and his head was pounding. He looked up at Lonnie and apologized for dragging him into the situation.

Lonnie placed his hand on Manuel's shoulder and assured him that God is truly in control of even the worst situations in which we find ourselves. He went on to say that even though he didn't know how, he was certain God had a plan for this very situation. With this, Manuel reluctantly granted Lonnie permission to speak with Mr. Reynolds. Lonnie called Jill in the HR office and asked if she would delay the termination until the very last hour of the workday, thus giving him time to brief Mr. Reynolds with some private information on Manuel's behalf.

When Lonnie shared the entire story with David Reynolds, he too broke down and wept openly. He truly wanted to help but was not certain of his legal rights given this very unique situation. He asked Lonnie to stay with him while he called the company's legal counsel for an opinion. The attorney stated that Reynolds wouldn't be breaking the law by making an exception, but that the best advice he could give was to stick with the policy and proceed with the termination. This would be the first but certainly not the last time Lonnie would see a business owner respond in a way that would surprise most of the employees of the company. After placing the phone back in the carriage, David Reynolds asked Lonnie to pray with him for God's guidance and protection in the decision he was about to make. Then with great wisdom, Mr. Reynolds called for Jill to join Lonnie and him in his office, where he laid out the following directive.

He started by saying that the exception he was about to make was just that, an exception to the rule, and not a change in the company's official critical incident drug policy. As a condition of his continued employment with the company, Manuel would be required to complete a drug education class. He would not be allowed to drive a company vehicle again until the class had been completed and he agreed to discontinue the alternative pain treatment. Manuel would be required to purchase the prescription pain medication for Madie, with the cost to be reimbursed through a payroll deduction from David Reynolds' personal account. In addition, Jill was instructed to work with Lonnie to help secure outside assistance for Manuel's family, with this assistance to be funded legally

yet confidentially through a Reynolds family foundation. Further, he stipulated that no one other than the three of them would have any knowledge of medical issues facing

...Jill was instructed to work with Lonnie to help secure outside assistance...

the family unless Manuel granted further confidentiality releases. He asked that Jill or Lonnie follow up with him within the next 24 hours once everything had been fully agreed upon by Manuel.

When Jill and Lonnie shared the news with Manuel, tears of joy streamed down his face. All three of them lifted their eyes heavenward and sincerely thanked God for intervening at such a critical time in their lives.

— 🦋 —

Leadership Transformers from Chapter Three

🦋 **Always follow through.** True leaders send out follow-up correspondence.

🦋 **People are different.** The people in your workplace come from various cultural, educational, environmental, and economic backgrounds that may cause them to see the world differently than you do.

🦋 **Confidentiality defines character.** Great leaders can be trusted with private information.

🦋 **People value privacy.** Even if you are the best leader in the city, sometimes subordinates are just not going to tell you everything that is going on in their lives.

🦋 **Right always prevails.** It is always right to do right, even if it flies in the face of conventional wisdom.

🦋 **Make exceptions thoughtfully.** When you make an exception to a policy, make sure all parties know it is an exception, not a new policy.

🦋 **Map out success.** When you make an exception to a policy, make sure a clear path to success is mapped out with definite accountability.

Leadership Ultimate Transformer Take Away

When people know they can trust you with their most private information, you will gain the right to lead them, with God's help, through the darkest times in their lives.

C-Changer's Transforming Thought

"A man had rather have a hundred lies told of him, than one truth which he does not wish should be told."

– Unknown

C-Change

Caregiving Transformers from
Chapter Three

🦋 **Make a prayer list.** Make a written prayer list of employees' needs and follow up with those in need for whom you pray.

🦋 **Workgroups are diverse.** Develop a deep understanding that your workplace mission field is richly and culturally diverse.

🦋 **Stories have sides.** Always remember that there are two sides to every story, and you should only respond after you have as clear a picture as possible of both sides.

🦋 **Hold your tongue.** Never breach an employee's confidence, even if you know doing so is in their best interest. (However, remember that you are required by law to breach confidentiality if there is an immediate safety risk to a person, or in the case of child abuse.)

🦋 **Listen with tenacity.** Develop "Strategic Listening" skills, and practice listening four times more than you talk.

🦋 **Let God judge.** Regardless of what an employee tells you, remember that you are there to care for them, not to judge them.

🦋 **Look for fresh ideas.** Be creative in looking for ways to help employees in crisis.

Caregiver's Ultimate Transformer Take Away

The heights your workplace ministry will reach are in direct proportion to your ability to hold a confidence.

Transformed by the Word

"Take control of what I say, O LORD, and keep my lips sealed."

– Psalms 141:3 (NLT)

CHAPTER FOUR

Transforming Principle Number Four

"COMPASSION"

The first few hectic weeks of his service as a corporate chaplain had now given way to a couple of months. The last several weeks had even become fairly routine for Lonnie, almost boring. As he made his rounds, he realized that learning the names of the employees was not the daunting task he had originally envisioned. As a matter of fact, he was surprised at just how easy it had been. He even found himself thinking how interesting it was that he already felt as though he knew the employees of his companies better than he had ever known the parishioners of the church he had served for so many years.

The last few weeks were so different than the first three. In fact, he was beginning to wonder if he was possibly doing something wrong. Sure, there were the routine prayer requests about aging parents in distant cities, the struggles of the single parents, and the discussions with employees about wayward children, sick pets, broken-down vehicles, and financial struggles. However, conspicuously absent were the major issues that set off his pager and caused him to react like a firefighter at Ladder Company 49. Lonnie was also battling a feeling of isolation as he drove between company locations day after day. This was so different from ministering in a church environment, and he was sometimes lonely.

He even made the same mistake that many rookie chaplains make as he lifted up the following prayer one day while riding home from making rounds at his companies:

"Lord, I must be doing something wrong. I don't feel as useful to these people as I did in the beginning. God, Johnny is really starting to get on my nerves. Would you please deal with him and get him off my back so I can care for the people in his department a little better? I'm a little discouraged that no one is coming to know Christ in my work. Sure, you have allowed me to help a few people through some tough issues, but the other chaplains on the team seem to have more spiritual activity in their mission fields than I do. What's up with that, God? Anyway, forgive me for being such a complainer, but I'd appreciate feeling a little more useful here, okay? I'm sorry, God. I guess I'm just a little tired. Just use me anyway you'd like, in Jesus' Name. Amen."

When he walked in the door at home, he greeted Sandy with a peck on the cheek. She looked him in the eye, rubbed his shoulders, and asked him why he looked so sad. He told her about his conversation with God, and how strange it was that he had never prayed a prayer like that when he served at the church. He had never really had a "pity party" in the past and didn't quite understand why he was having one now. Sandy reassured him how special he was and asked if he had shared these feelings with his ministry supervisor, Mike. He admitted that he hadn't because he didn't want to look weak, but that it might be a good idea and he would consider giving him a call after dinner.

Mike had been around the block, both as a chaplain and now a senior managing chaplain for the ministry they served. When Lonnie relayed his feelings, Mike initially let out a hearty laugh. This was not the reaction he was expecting. As a matter of fact, it made him a little angry. However, as Mike unfolded stories of other chaplains who had gone through almost exactly the same emotions, Lonnie began to settle down

and realize that Mike's words were really reassuring. It was comforting to know that his thoughts and feelings were a normal part of the first few months of the chaplain acclimation process, especially for those who enter corporate chaplaincy after having served as senior pastors of larger churches. However, Mike ended their conversation with the following warning that really made Lonnie think: "You should be careful what you pray for, big boy, because God really is listening, and He has a way of giving us the things we ask for."

"You should be careful what you pray for, big boy, because God really is listening..."

Another 24 hours passed. Sandy and Lonnie were sitting on the front porch after dinner, watching their kids catch fireflies in jelly jars. Out of the stillness of the summer night, Lonnie's pager sounded with its *chirp, vibrate,* startling both of them into the reality of the present. The number in the pager was his own, which meant he had a voice message waiting for him on the system server. As he dialed the number and entered his ID code, the computer responded, "You have one unheard message. Press one to listen to current message." He pressed the "1" button on his phone and the automated voice intoned the time the message came in. Then he began to hear the excited voice of the trucking company's dispatcher asking him to call as soon as possible. There had been a terrible accident!

Immediately his mind displayed graphic visions of a horrible truck accident. Little did he know how wrong this mental image would be. When he called to get the details, he was surprised to learn that there had not been a truck accident at all. The situation was worse than any truck accident he could have imagined. There had been a tragedy in the life of a local pick up and delivery driver he had gotten to know very well over the last couple of months named Tommy. Tommy was a family man who truly loved his wife and two kids. His son was away at college and his daughter, a real daddy's girl, was a junior at the local high school. She and her best girlfriend were riding in a car with a boy from the neighborhood, when every parent's nightmare occurred. On a back country road on the way to taking the girls home, the boy had lost control of the car in a curve and hit a tree. The neighbor's girl that Tommy had watched grow up with his daughter over the past sixteen years was dead, and his own little girl lay near death in the intensive care unit of

the local medical center. The boy who was driving was un-hurt and being questioned by the authorities at the county sheriff's office.

He dropped his head and prayed for every-one connected to the accident...

That swirling feeling in his head was back, and ironically, one of Lonnie's first thoughts was of Mike saying, "...be careful what you pray for, big boy..." He dropped his head and prayed for everyone connected to the accident, kissed Sandy and held his kids tight before rushing for his car and making his way to the hospital.

He was not prepared for what he saw as he entered the parking lot of the hospital. About fifty kids from the local high school were already gathered outside the entrance. They were somewhat angry that they hadn't gotten any information about Katie and had been asked to wait outside the hospital for further word. The hospital had only sent them outside because of the size of the group and the concern that the numbers might grow as the evening went on. But the kids had taken the action personally and believed it was only because of their youth.

The students and friends in the group were becoming more hostile as Lonnie made his way toward them. As he approached the group, he asked if they were there because of the accident. One of the boys, thinking Lonnie worked for the hospital, offered an obscenity followed by the assertion that they deserved some answers regarding their friend. Lonnie quickly let them know who he was and that as soon as he could get some information, he would come back and let them know what was going on.

When he reached the area right outside the intensive care door, he saw Tommy and his wife, Connie. Connie was crying and emotionally distraught.

Tommy, the strapping truck driver, had the pale look of a person who had just seen a ghost. Lonnie silently began to pray, asking God to give him the words for this terrible situation. The only thing he could think to do was put out his arms. Both Tommy and Connie fell into them with a thud. Lonnie felt the atmosphere of the moment hanging with a dreamlike quality, as if time was suspended. Without saying a word, he simply embraced the couple and joined them in their uncontrollable tears.

The few minutes that they held each other seemed like an hour. When they reluctantly released each other, Lonnie asked about Katie's condition. They had not yet seen her. A doctor had come out to tell them she had sustained head and neck injuries and was in critical condition, but they would be allowed to see her as soon as possible.

Because he had been pre-certified at the hospital, Lonnie's Clergy Pass allowed him to enter the intensive care unit to speak with a nurse. New privacy rules had made it unlawful for hospital personnel to share patient information with unauthorized people, so Lonnie took out a business card and began to write a sentence on the back. He asked Tommy to read it when he pressed the voice record button on his cell phone. "This is Tommy Fisher. The man playing this recorder is my minister, Lonnie Pepper. You have my permission to give him information about the condition of my daughter Katie." With this, Lonnie made his way into the ICU and played the message for the charge nurse.

After telling Lonnie she thought she had seen everything, she whipped out a form for the Fishers to sign, gave it to Lonnie, and sent him back to the waiting area. He returned with the form, and the nurse gave him a medical update on Katie's condition. She was indeed clinging to life. Lonnie asked if he could bring Katie's parents in to see her. The nurse walked down the hall to one of the glass-enclosed areas. She was gone for what seemed to be an hour. When she returned, she said Lonnie could bring the parents in for only a moment before Katie was taken into surgery. There was a lump in his stomach the size of a watermelon as he walked out to get Tommy and Connie. As the three of them walked silently back into the ICU, Lonnie was praying for God's healing, strength, courage, and mercy.

When they looked at Katie's unconscious body hooked up to all kinds of monitors, the only thing Lonnie could think of was his mental picture of Jesus in the New Testament calling for the children to come to Him. He held on tightly to the hands of Tommy and Connie as they looked at their daughter and cried. Lonnie couldn't help but think of his own kids at home, playing in the yard when he last saw them. Soon a surgical team arrived and whisked Katie to the OR. When Lonnie walked back into the ICU waiting room with Tommy and Connie, a group of their family members had assembled. They were waiting to hear news of Katie's condition and offer care and support. Lonnie's mind went back to the kids outside. He told Tommy about them and asked his permission to tell the kids what was going on. Tommy was touched that they were there and readily gave his permission.

As Lonnie walked out the front door of the hospital, he noticed that the group had now grown to more than seventy-five kids. The same boy that had earlier voiced the obscenity now hollered out that the preacher was back and for everyone to quiet down.

Lonnie started by telling them how proud he was of them for caring so much about a friend that they would camp outside the hospital. He sent them greetings and thanks from Katie's parents. He then let them know that Katie was in surgery and really could use their prayers. He asked them for permission to pray with them right then. Girls were crying and the guys were trying to look tough, but every-

He asked them for permission to pray with them right then.

one simply lowered their heads as a sign for Lonnie to pray. He told them he would send a friend to help them in a little while and would do his best to keep them informed about Katie's progress.

As he walked away from the group, he called the youth minister at the church he and Sandy had recently joined and asked him if he would mind coming out to minister to the kids. The young man was all too happy to help out and assured Lonnie he could be there in less than a half hour. As Lonnie made his way back to the ICU waiting area to care for the family, he couldn't help but entertain a fleeting thought that even though he had often read stories in the paper about cases like this, they were always somewhere else, for someone else. They weren't supposed to be so close to home...not in *his* mission field.

The operation this day was only the first of six Katie would survive over the next four days. Over the course of the next fourteen days, Lonnie provided continuous care for Katie's family. He would always go by the hospital first thing in the morning, often taking Hardee's sausage biscuits for family members who had camped out in the waiting room all night. He would stop back by during the day, and he was always there to sit with Tommy and Connie when the surgeries were taking place. He was blessed to enter into deep and abiding ministry conversations with many members of Tommy's family through this entire process. Some even entered into personal relationships with Christ. Eventually Katie recovered physically, in answer to many prayers by hundreds of people. Gaining the basic coping skills necessary to deal with the emotional scars of losing her friend would take much longer.

More opportunities for ministry with this case

continued for Lonnie, as the civil and criminal court cases for the young man driving the car on that fateful day weaved their way through the judicial system.

One evening toward the end of the summer when once again Lonnie and Sandy were on the front porch watching the kids catch fireflies in jelly jars, he prayed for his children's safety and marveled at how God works in the lives of ordinary people who find themselves caught up in extraordinary circumstances.

Leadership Transformers from Chapter Four

🦋 **Rest during downtime.** Sometimes the leader's life will become routine. Gather emotional and physical strength during these times.

🦋 **Develop firefighter's mentality.** Respond quickly when a crisis occurs.

🦋 **Get facts fast.** When called into a major crisis, quickly collect as many facts as possible.

🦋 **Leaders truly care.** Great leaders demonstrate heartfelt compassion during a crisis.

🦋 **Acknowledge outside forces.** Keep in mind that there are always secondary parties to every crisis.

🦋 **Share the load.** Focus on the central problem and be ready to delegate the minor details of a crisis to a qualified associate.

🦋 **Finish the race.** Continue to work on a crisis until it draws to a natural conclusion.

Leader's Ultimate Transformer Take Away

Great leaders develop compassion skills and use them when crises occur.

C-Changer's Transforming Thought

"When a man has compassion for others, God has compassion for him."

– The Talmud

Caregiving Transformers from Chapter Four

🦋 **Work your plan.** Work your own ministry plan, and stay away from the peer comparison game.

🦋 **Seek advice fast.** Never hesitate to call on a friend or supervisor when things seem abnormal.

🦋 **God answers prayer.** Be careful what you ask of God; you just might get it.

🦋 **Return pages quickly.** Always return pages immediately. Someone is counting on your quick response.

🦋 **Register for credentials.** Most hospitals and jails in your town will require advance registration in order for chaplains to receive access. Get these matters handled before a crisis occurs.

🦋 **Care for others.** Keep in mind that a major crisis gives you the opportunity to minister to many people outside the workplace to which you have been assigned.

🦋 **Visit hospitals daily.** Remember to visit the hospital daily until the member of your mission field is released.

Caregiver's Ultimate Transformer Take Away

Compassion is the fuel that drives the caregiver's heart. Ask God often to fill your tank with the high octane fruit of the Spirit.

Transformed by the Word

"But if anyone has enough money to live well and sees a brother or sister in need and refuses to help—how can God's love be in that person? Dear children, let us stop just saying we love each other; let us really show it by our actions."

– 1 John 3:18 (NLT)

CHAPTER FIVE

Transforming Principle Number Five

"CONTROL"

L onnie left his house early on a warm summer morning to meet an employee at a local Starbucks. He felt thankful to be serving God in such an awesome and diverse mission field. He had left home particularly early that morning in order to meet with Austin, a young supervisor who had paged him and requested a meeting to discuss some minor personality issues he was having with a subordinate. Lonnie realized the best thing to do in this care giving session was to listen and possibly offer some relationship advice. He knew his role was that of the chaplain and not some kind of business consultant. However, the opportunity to have an impact on Austin's life could pay great ministry dividends in the future. His simple care giving and encouraging role now could help shape a young man who seemed destined for greater management potential.

Lonnie had observed Austin's interactions with other employees and had become convinced that the young man could have a future as an executive who would lead with a "servant leader" mentality. This was a concept he had noticed as he continued to study the New Testament. Since becoming a workplace chaplain, God had revealed case study after case study to him of Jesus as the ultimate servant leader. He was amazed that his new role as a corporate chaplain had opened up new vistas in the scriptures to him. Hardly a day went by when God didn't show him a nugget of truth that he had never seen before. More often than not, Lonnie was able to share it at just the right time with an employee who was struggling with a problem and openly seeking some form of spiritual counsel. What he had learned about the providence of God, both in seminary and through his own study of the Bible, was more real in his new work than he would have ever imagined. All of a sudden he was visually, and mentally, seeing God's providence, not just in the great events of life, but also in the most minor events of the day. He often wondered why he hadn't recognized this so acutely before.

Many times Lonnie found himself almost instinctively encouraging an employee in a crisis not to lose heart with the phrase, "Somehow this will work out because God really is in control, and we aren't." This wasn't his way of handing out an easy answer to a very complex or

"Somehow this will all work out because God really is in control and we aren't."

debilitating challenge. He was mature enough in his faith to know that sometimes there just was no other reasonable answer. As things continued to be rocky in the Fab Shop with Johnny, Lonnie found himself inwardly and silently repeating this same phrase. The situation had become a matter of frequent prayer and increasing frustration for him, but deep down inside he knew that, "God is in control, and this will work out somehow."

Lonnie soon learned that informal communication "grapevines" really do exist in every company. He sensed that he was rapidly becoming the subject of the beating of jungle drums within the ranks of employees. The word was spreading in each of his companies of his ability to help people with their problems. With each beat of the drum, it seemed that more employees were opening up during his rounds, but the point was about to be brought home in an unusual way on this particular day.

When Lonnie arrived at the Starbucks, Austin was waiting for him at a table outside, already nursing a Grande Mocha. It was obvious he had pulled the table away from others in order to provide some privacy.

"Are you sure everything I'm about to tell you will be confidential?"

Austin motioned for Lonnie to go inside to order while he saved their spot. When he returned, Austin's opening question made it apparent that the conversation was not going to be about his skills as a supervisor. Lonnie had learned that the now familiar question, "Are you sure everything I'm about to tell you will be confidential?", usually signaled some deep and potentially paralyzing crisis in the life of an employee. Lonnie gave him the assurance that it would, and Austin lowered his head and began in a soft and repentant tone.

He started by telling Lonnie about his wife and two small kids and his love for them. He went on to say he hadn't seen them for over a week and that inside he felt like he was dying. Lonnie waited for the other shoe to drop, thinking he was about to hear the story of how an affair was about to destroy another family. He had dealt with several of these situations as a pastor, but this wasn't the case for Austin. No, Lonnie was about to hear a much different story from this upwardly mobile young supervisor, who from all outward appearances looked like he had the world by the tail. He said it had all started out so innocently as they were having a family cookout with some friends from work. Austin was on the deck with a guy from the sales team, drinking a beer, smoking a cigar, and cooking some steaks. With all the subtlety of a slithering snake, his so-called buddy whipped out a pipe and asked him to take a ride with some "fun smoke." Little did Austin know that his first drag on the pipe would ultimately bring his world tumbling down like a spring avalanche in the Alps.

Austin had smoked some pot back in college and

thought that was what the pipe contained. He should have known better, but he just found himself caught up in the moment. Before Austin knew it, he had taken his first hit on a crack pipe. The initial high was unbelievable, but it didn't last. The shame and guilt that followed were profound.

Austin would later find the cycles were always the same - use of the drug, in search of that first euphoric high which had been seared in his mind the first time he smoked it on the deck - followed by a period of great emotional shame and guilt, during which he always swore he would never touch the stuff again. The sad reality was that psychological triggers were already locked in his brain - the taste of a certain brand of beer, the aroma of a steak on the grill, or the smell of a burning cigar. Without fail, he would begin craving that original high once again and looking for a way to get his hands on the drug.

It had been about a year since his first use. In the beginning Austin went almost a month between the cycles of use, shame, guilt, trigger, extreme desire, and then re-use. Back then he was able to hide it from everyone, including his wife. The money he spent on the drug was hardly missed. Now however, things had dramatically changed. Over the last six months, Austin's entire world had come unglued. To support an almost daily habit, he had liquidated his retirement account, totally tapped out the equity line on his house, and finally cashed the savings bonds he and his wife, Nicole, had saved for the kids' education. Nicole found out what was going on about a month ago and was totally devastated. Austin begged for her forgiveness and promised that he was "cured". Based on that commitment, she agreed to stay with him, but just last week he fell again. This time he was so desperate for cash to buy the drug, that he sold his wedding band for twenty dollars. Nicole took the kids and went to live with her parents in Denver.

Austin could no longer hide his emotions and looked at Lonnie with the eyes of a person without a friend in the world and nowhere to turn. He thought he had been effectively hiding what was going on from his boss and everyone else at work. However, now he was hitting bottom. The only thing that kept Austin from taking his own life the night before was the fleeting hope that the chaplain might be able to help. The irony in this thought was Austin's memory from the chaplain orientation day, when something deep inside was telling him that this guy just might be able to help him. That very day he left work early and went out and partied late into the night, telling Nicole he was out of town on company business. What a difference a few months can make, he thought, while miserably rubbing his pounding temples. Now, as Austin sat there broken, with a level of shame and remorse he had never imagined he would feel, he was pinning all of his hope on a guy he had only known for a couple of months. He was sure Lonnie thought he was just a big loser.

Lonnie's first words shocked Austin so much that he lifted his head in disbelief. In a soft and quiet voice, Lonnie simply said, "Austin, I love you, but God loves you more than I do. If I can have your permission, I want to share with you how I think God can help you work through all of this." At first Austin didn't know how to react. Lonnie didn't say another word while he waited

Lonnie's first words shocked Austin so much that he lifted his head in disbelief.

for him to respond. After what seemed like an hour of silence, Austin finally agreed to do anything that Lonnie thought might help him. Lonnie started by telling him the truth about where he stood spiritually and how God was ready at this very moment to intervene. He talked about the fact that Jesus was the real, living, God of the universe and how Austin's only hope for the future was to immediately enter into a personal relationship with Him. Lonnie went on to explain that the rest of Austin's life would need to be a day by day, hour by hour, minute by minute, and second by second dependence on Jesus Christ. As they prayed together, Austin surrendered his life to Jesus and actually begged for that second-by-second relationship with Him.

Next, Lonnie recommended that he and Austin visit with Jill in HR and tell her what was going on. Lonnie encouraged him to enter the company's drug rehab program. Lastly, Lonnie asked for Austin's permission to call Nicole to request a time for the three of them to talk together on the phone, in the hopes of opening a dialog and beginning the process of reconciliation. He advised Austin to use that opportunity to tell Nicole about his new relationship with Jesus, his remorse for the past, and his desire and willingness to earn back her trust, even if it took the rest of his life.

Their meeting finally drew to a close and Lonnie followed Austin to the plant. Austin began to talk to Jesus himself, thanking Him and asking for the help he was going to need so desperately during the difficult days that lay ahead.

— —

Leadership Transformers from Chapter Five

🦋 **Lead through service.** Servant leadership dates back to the time of Christ. It was powerfully effective then and is still so today.

🦋 **Powerful leadership principles.** The Bible contains leadership principles that can be powerful in 21st century management situations.

🦋 **Harness the grapevine.** Communication grapevines are active in every business. Harness the knowledge of how they work, and use it positively as part of your management strategy.

🦋 **Face the facts.** Illegal drugs are used in the workplace. Leaders who educate themselves about this productivity killer can become positive agents for change.

🦋 **Perception isn't reality.** Issues facing the employees under the span of our leadership are not always as they appear on the surface.

🦋 **Bad stuff happens.** Sometimes our best and brightest subordinates can find themselves in deep, dark holes, where only God can help them recover.

🦋 **Exercise your heart.** Great leaders can develop faith-based emotional shock absorbers to help handle the trauma associated with managing people.

Leader's Ultimate Transformer Take Away

Servant leaders harness the true power of the universe and can have a dramatic impact on any company in any industry.

C-Changer's Transforming Thought

"Mama says, we aren't never in control of nothing and she's always right about that."

– Forrest Gump

Caregiving Transformers from Chapter Five

🦋 **Search for wisdom.** Workplace caregivers should daily study the Bible to look for nuggets of wisdom for use in the workplace.

🦋 **God is working.** God's providence is often seen in the little aspects of everyday life. Always be on the lookout for ways God is manifesting Himself in the workplace.

🦋 **Never be surprised.** The power of addiction can get a grip on the most unlikely people in your mission field.

🦋 **God knows all.** God is in control, and we are not.

🦋 **Word spreads fast.** As you continue to help more and more people in your mission field, word will spread and your influence for the cause of Christ will grow.

🦋 **Respond in love.** When a person reveals to you their deepest, darkest, ugliest life secret, always respond with the love of Christ as if you are listening and responding for Him.

🦋 **Saturate spirituality now.** The only hope for a drug-addicted employee is for them to start their rehab process by entering into a day by day, hour by hour, minute by minute, second by second relationship with Jesus Christ.

Caregiver's Ultimate Transformer Take Away

God is in control and we are not; praise be to God!

Transformed by the Word

"For the earth is the Lord's, and everything in it."
– I Cor. 10:26 (NLT)

CHAPTER SIX

Transforming Principle Number Six

"CONSISTENCY"

Lonnie truly felt that his role as a workplace chaplain was flowing smoothly. As he looked back at the process which had brought him to this point, he could see how all the pieces of the puzzle were finally coming together. There were times in the early stages of the interview and hiring process he thought the ministry he was now serving was going a bit overboard. In the very beginning he was almost insulted that the strength of his resume had not caused the ministry to recruit him like a first round NBA draft pick. However, this hadn't been the case at all. There had been numerous phone and personal interviews. Sandy was even subjected to a joint interview with him. There were personality assessments and criminal

and credit background checks. He remembered thinking all of this was a bit much. He was Lonnie Pepper,
for crying out loud - DR. Lonnie Pepper. Now, however, he had come to understand that this had been
shameful personal pride, and that God was helping
him work through it before he could be truly useful in
workplace ministry. The employees didn't need Reverend Lonnie, the great preacher, or Lonnie Pepper, the
guy who graduated near the top of his seminary class.
No, they could have cared less about his doctorate.
He was now aware that some of the very best chaplains, and even managers, on the team were not there
because of theological pedigrees and fancy degrees.
They were there because God Himself had allowed
the building blocks of their lives to lead directly to the
point where He could entrust them with the spiritual
care of employees.

Lonnie had also thought that the initial training
was a bit intense. In addition, the fact that he would
have to complete another hundred hours of continuing education training within his first year in order to
qualify for a good raise was, at first, a cause for concern. All of these early impressions had now reversed

and become points of respect and admiration for the team he had joined. Lonnie was rapidly realizing he had been allowed, and even chosen, to serve in one of the greatest mission fields on Earth.

He was looking forward to attending an upcoming chaplain training meeting in Florida, where he would have the opportunity to spend some quality time with the other chaplains on the team, as well as to learn some new skills. The ministry he served took all of the chaplains out of the field three times a year for a 3-day breather and time of decompression. But the events included more than that. There was also a focus on valuable continued training and an opportunity for just plain fun, as the chaplains became acquainted with other chaplains experiencing the same issues in the field. He had heard stories about how great the meetings were, and he was looking forward to attending his first. His only concern about the meeting was the fact that he had been selected to room with a chaplain from Atlanta named Jerry. One of the rookies was always selected for this dubious honor, an initiation of sorts. He had been told that Jerry was the seventh chaplain to join the team many years ago and referred to himself as "007, Licensed to Thrill". He was known to be a great chaplain, yet he had a colorful personality and took great pleasure in the running folklore about his hazing of one of the new guys at each meeting. Lonnie was a good sport and thought to himself that someone like Jerry just might be able to relate to the problems he continued to have with Johnny. He was willing to bet Jerry would offer some good advice.

Normally Lonnie made rounds at Reynolds on Mondays and Thursdays during the day, and on Wednesday afternoons and evenings in order to visit second shift employees. He learned that the employees became comfortable with his routine and actually looked for him at these specific times. Because of a couple of hospital cases from earlier in the week, he had gotten off his regular rounds schedule. This happened rarely, but when it did, there would usually be an employee or two that would remind him about it with a comment like, "Hey, I missed you yesterday. Where were you?"

The first time that happened, it caught Lonnie a little off guard. He had now experienced firsthand what he had heard in training about how important it was to be consistent with his rounds schedule. He quickly came to realize that being missed was a good thing, and often the employees were really counting on him to stop by their workstations for a very brief moment of encouragement. It was not at all uncommon for Lonnie to hear a comment like, "I was going to page you about something last night, but I knew I would see you today, so I just waited." Brief care sessions with employees who were dealing with minor issues were becoming more common now. He had learned that often more time was needed to discuss an issue with employees than was available at the workstation. In such cases, he was careful to make an appointment to come back and visit with the employee at break or lunch time when it wouldn't interfere with their work assignments.

There were rare cases when Lonnie had to make the call to encourage an employee to leave the production line for safety reasons. This happened one day when a supervisor paged Lonnie and asked him to come by the plant to check on a young warehouse forklift driver named Jimmy. Jimmy's supervisor noticed that he was unusually quiet when he clocked in for work that morning. He was not his usual happy-go-lucky self. Another employee saw him just sitting on his forklift, staring into space like a robot. The supervisors in the plant had received a special orientation session regarding the chaplain program. They knew they could page the chaplain if they recognized a need with a subordinate. There had already been a couple of minor cases where Lonnie had been called in to offer some employee care in similar situations. This time the supervisor knew something was wrong with the young man but wasn't sure what it might be. He didn't want to either under or overreact to the situation. He knew that if he paged Lonnie, he would hear right back from him and be able to get a quick second opinion.

All the chaplains in the organization Lonnie served maintained a ten minute page return guarantee. When the employees Lonnie cared for called his pager, they heard, "Hello, this is your chaplain, Lonnie. At the sound of the tone, please press '1' to leave me your phone number or '2' to leave me a voice message. If I haven't called you back within the next ten minutes, please page me again. I wouldn't want to miss your call." The guarantee was impressive to employees who had become accustomed to poor customer service or being trapped in a "voice mail dungeon", never to hear back from the person they were trying to reach. This particular supervisor had seen Lonnie joking with Jimmy at various times while in the plant making rounds. He thought Lonnie might have some insight about the situation.

He thought Lonnie might have some insight about the situation.

Lonnie was on the phone with the supervisor within a few minutes of receiving the page. He had no idea what might be going on with the young man, but he asked the supervisor to keep an eye on Jimmy until he got there. Because he was already in the plant, he could be at the forklift on line fourteen in a matter of minutes.

Lonnie approached Jimmy just as if he was making regular rounds, but he could tell something wasn't right. He made eye contact, waved his hand, and yelled in order to be heard over the clanging machinery, "Good morning," yet Jimmy sat motionless and unresponsive. As he lifted a silent prayer and walked over to the forklift, Lonnie gently laid his hand on Jimmy's arm. This startled Jimmy somewhat, and he looked at Lonnie as if he had never seen him before.

Lonnie wasn't sure what was wrong. Was it possible Jimmy was on drugs, or maybe having an allergic reaction to a prescription medication? Jimmy was only nineteen, and this was his first full-time job since leaving high school. Lonnie looked at Jimmy and simply asked, "Hey Jimmy, what's going on this morning? You don't seem like yourself." In a soft voice, Jimmy said, "My baby sister was killed in a car wreck last night." Almost reflexively, Lonnie said, "Wow, that's terrible. What are you doing here?" Jimmy replied that everything was so crazy at home overnight, that he just didn't know what else to do or where else to go. Lonnie asked him to climb down from the forklift, clock out, and walk across the street to the Hardee's with him.

As they sat in the booth across from one another, Jimmy told Lonnie the whole story of what happened the night before. He and his parents had gone to bed around ten-thirty. Sometime around eleven, a state trooper rang the doorbell and told them his sister had been killed in a two-car accident over on Highway 98. Jimmy had stayed awake the rest of the night. When morning came he knew he could come to the plant, see his friends, and get his head back together. For some reason, when he had walked into the plant, he had just zoned out and didn't want to talk about what had happened. He went on to tell Lonnie he had never been to a funeral home or a church, and he didn't even have a suit to wear to his sister's funeral.

Lonnie was able to get him to tell some stories about his sister and family. He learned that it was just the four of them, and they had always been very close. His sister was only seventeen. She had gone for ice cream with some friends after work and was on the way home when the accident occurred.

Lonnie prayed with Jimmy and let him know that he would be there to help him get through this terrible situation. He told Jimmy he would help him get a suit later that day. Lonnie asked permission to tell the folks at the plant what had happened, and then asked if he could give Jimmy a ride home and have one of the guys at the plant return his car to him later that afternoon. Jimmy had begun the grieving process. That process offered Lonnie and Jimmy an opportunity to build their lives together in ways that would be unusually fulfilling in the years to come.

— ❦ —

Leadership Transformers from Chapter Six

🦋 **Recruit with care.** Leaders develop great recruiting and interviewing skills and procedures.

🦋 **Learn for life.** Great leaders develop and encourage continuing education training for their staff members and themselves.

🦋 **Consistency pays dividends.** Team members will almost always over deliver for a leader who is consistent in making decisions and carrying out directives.

🦋 **Watch for signs.** When an employee is not acting normally, be sensitive and ready to respond with help.

🦋 **Nowhere else.** Recognize that sometimes employees will come to work while experiencing major crises because they feel safe at work. They may be disoriented and not know where else to go or what else to do.

🦋 **Consistency develops trust.** Consistent leaders develop trusting relationships with subordinates.

🦋 **Crises create change.** When a major crisis occurs in the life of one employee, it will almost always have an effect on the performance and morale of the entire team.

Leader's Ultimate Transformer Take Away

Be who you are all day long, even when no one is looking. It will become natural to function with consistency regardless of the circumstances.

C-Changer's Transforming Thought

"One does not surrender a life in an instant. That which is life long can only be surrendered in a lifetime."
— *Jim Elliot, 20th century missionary martyr*

Caregiving Transformers from Chapter Six

🦋 **Let pride fall.** God has to shave down our pride before we can be totally useful to him.

🦋 **Concern is visible.** Employees could care less how much you know, until you demonstrate how much you care.

🦋 **Always get away.** Workplace caregivers need to retreat from the field with peers, in order to decompress their minds and emotions from the trials of the work.

🦋 **Employees crave consistency.** As a leader and caregiver, be consistent.

🦋 **Keep your cool.** Until you know all the facts, approach employees who are potentially in crisis as if everything were normal.

🦋 **Watch for trouble.** When you determine an employee may be at risk of harming himself or others, take immediate action.

🦋 **Expect the unexpected.** As a workplace caregiver, be prepared for things to be unlike what you anticipated.

Caregiver's Ultimate Transformer Take Away

One of the most important things you can do as a workplace caregiver is to be totally consistent in what you say, what you do, what you think and, most importantly, who you are.

Transformed by the Word

"I have fought a good fight, I have finished the race, and I have remained faithful."

– 2 Timothy 4:7 (NLT)

CHAPTER SEVEN

Transforming Principle Number Seven

"CONVERSION"

A couple of months had passed since Jimmy lost his sister, and he was progressing well through the five primary stages of the grieving process. Lonnie had gotten really close to Jimmy and had learned a great deal from what this young man and his family had been through.

Lonnie was getting ready to take his family back home for vacation in a few weeks. He had just returned from a three-day chaplain training event, and it had been exactly what he needed. Rooming with Jerry was a piece of cake. After all the build up and joking, Jerry turned out to be the perfect guy to take a new chaplain under his wing. Lonnie was glad he had been the one from his initial training class selected for the "hazing." Being with so many chaplains like him, gathered in one place from all over the country, was an awesome experience that he would never forget. He already found himself longing for the next meeting. Lonnie had made new friendships, renewed acquaintances with the guys from his training class, and discovered that the challenges he faced in the field were pretty much universal. It was also good to see Chris again. Lonnie marveled at how God worked though Chris' life to enrich the lives of the chaplains. The meeting also gave him an opportunity to spend time with the organization's leadership and hear presentations about the future direction of the work.

There was an awards banquet on the first night. Chaplains were recognized for various service milestones. Chaplains who attained five years of service were presented a specially designed gold ring with a ruby stone, encrusted with a gold cross. There was another award with a funny name that would be in his own future. It was called the "Dog Year Award" and was given to employees of the organization who had completed a full year's service. The theory behind the award was that serving one year as a chaplain was the equivalent of seven years in any other type of ministry. Lonnie already knew this to be true with just several months under his belt. Other awards included "Chaplain of the Quarter", "Soul Winner of the Quarter", and the "Stealth Bomber Award", which was given to the chaplain who had the most impact in his mission field while hardly being seen or heard from in the process.

One award he found to be particularly amusing was the coveted "Skunk Tie Award". A number of years ago, a leader in the organization had come across this hideously ugly necktie with little black and white skunks printed in the design. The entire management team voted on the award, which was presented to the chaplain who was deemed to have dealt with the "stinkiest", or most difficult, case since the last meeting. The chaplain who won the award at the last training meeting was asked to make the presentation to the current winner, who then wore the tie for the balance of the evening and was responsible for bringing it to the next meeting.

The next day there was a half day of classroom training presented by Dr. Carlisle and Chris that, providentially, hit on the exact topics Lonnie had come there hoping to settle. In the afternoon and evening, a special outing had been planned at a local theme park where the chaplains basically played like little kids at a birthday party. The final day of training included a half day of classroom training before they headed back to their respective cities.

Lonnie returned home from training with plenty of stories to tell Sandy and felt reenergized for whatever lay ahead of him in his mission field. Little did Lonnie know that he would be coming home to the most challenging ministry case he had faced, and where else would it unfold but in the Fab Shop where he had been made to feel like an exile.

It all started on a quiet Monday morning. Employees were settling into the regular routine of their jobs,

like any other new workweek. Barbara Jones was a middle-aged African-American lady who worked in the Fab Shop as a welder. She was as big and tough as any of the men,

As far as Lonnie could tell, she was the only Christian in the shop.

with one major exception. As far as Lonnie could tell,

she was the only Christian in the shop. She was also the only one there who ever really talked to Lonnie, and he was certain she was the only one that wasn't intimidated by Johnny.

Lonnie had enjoyed talking with her around the lunchroom table about her days in the Army where she had apprenticed as a welder. Barbara had eventually become one of the best welders in the entire service. Her superiors in the Army had always encouraged her to become a trainer and move up through the ranks, but she was perfectly content to simply be the best at her craft and enjoy a simpler life devoted to God and country. She had never married and retired after twenty years of service. Barbara returned to her hometown and proudly went to work for the company from which her father had retired almost ten years ago. She was clearly the best welder in the Fab Shop and enjoyed the respect of everyone there, including Johnny.

On this particular Monday morning, as Johnny walked by her equipment station and grunted out a hoarse "Mornin', Barb," she said something he had never heard from her in the past. "Johnny, I've got a headache." By this time Johnny had walked past her station. He looked back over his shoulder with an expression on his face that said, "Sure you have a headache; it's Monday." Before he had time to fully turn back around, Barbara had fallen to the floor and was totally unconscious. Though he hadn't treated Lonnie well, Johnny was a professional and very good at his job. He immediately gathered his thoughts and yelled for someone to call "9II".

As the EMS workers sped away with sirens blazing and lights flashing, Joe from Safety paged Lonnie to the hospital. When Lonnie arrived, Barbara was already in the ICU, hooked up to all kinds of life support machines. The charge nurse recognized Lonnie from all the time he had spent there when Tommy's daughter was injured in the car accident last spring. She told him the doctor had given instructions to contact Barbara's family members and ask them to come as soon as possible. Lonnie told her that someone from the HR department at Reynolds was already on the case.

Just then Barbara's father, Walter Jones, walked up and asked about his daughter's condition. The nurse asked Lonnie to stay with Mr. Jones while she went for the doctor. Looking down the hall a few moments later, they guessed by his green scrubs and the stethoscope hanging around his neck that this must be the doctor coming toward them now.

Dr. Bryant walked slowly, which signaled the worst. As Lonnie and Mr. Jones identified themselves with a quick handshake, Mr. Jones' voice quivered as he choked out the words, "How's my little girl?" Sadly the doctor informed them that Barbara had experienced a brain aneurysm and the only thing keeping her alive were the life support machines. He asked Mr. Jones to sign a consent form to authorize the disconnection of the machines. Mr. Jones' knees buckled as he steadied himself against the nurse's station on one side and against Lonnie on the other. He could only whisper, "My dear Lord...how could this be...she was so healthy and vibrant...she's my little girl..." Lonnie asked Dr. Bryant to give them some private time together.

Lonnie walked with Mr. Jones to the hospital chapel, where they sat, cried, and prayed together. Mr. Jones told Lonnie that Barbara had spoken of him often. They had even prayed for Lonnie during their evening family devotions, because she didn't like the way Johnny had been treating him. Then Mr. Jones, a deeply spiritual man, looked Lonnie in the eye and asked a penetrating question. "Chaplain, if I sign those forms for the doctor to disconnect the machines, would it be the same as me killing my little girl?" As tenderly as spoken words would allow, Lonnie reminded him that God alone is in control of when we are born and when we will die. Whether the machines were hooked up or

...God alone is in control of when we are born and when we will die.

not, only God would decide when Barbara's spirit would leave this earth and be with Him in Heaven. "She may even be with Him there now. We just don't know, but one thing is certain. Your decision today will not keep God from healing her if it is His will or taking her home to be with Him." With that he rose to his feet, and they both made their way to find the doctor. Lonnie stood with Mr. Jones as he signed the forms by Barbara's bed.

The last time Mr. Jones had been in a hospital, he was standing by the bed of his wife of fifty-two years at the very moment she passed away following a stroke. Now it was his little girl. They asked Dr. Bryant how long Barbara would live after the machines were taken away. He said it could be a matter of minutes or it could be longer; they never really knew. Mr. Jones must have been thinking out loud, although he was looking right at Barbara when he muttered, "If I've done the right thing, she's already with Jesus." He kissed her on the cheek, and then he and Lonnie stepped to the corner of the room.

Lonnie prayed with Mr. Jones as the doctor and nurse disconnected all of the machines. After a couple of minutes, Dr. Bryant came to their side and softly informed them that Barbara had passed away only seconds after the machines had been disconnected.

Lonnie spent the next few hours with the Jones family in their home. He hadn't been there long before their minister, Reverend Lucas Pollard, arrived. Extended family members and many people from the church began to come in as well. When he knew Mr. Jones and his family would be well cared for, Lonnie quickly made his way to the plant. Reynolds employees were like a big family, and he knew Barbara's death would be a major blow. Lonnie called his ministry supervisor,

Mike, to request prayer and to give him a briefing on the case. Mike immediately decided to have Ray Wilson, a chaplain on the team in Hinnantsville, a town about thirty miles to the south, come to the plant and help Lonnie work with the grieving employees.

Knowing that rumors would be running around the plant about what might have happened to Barbara, Lonnie asked Mr. Jones' permission and phoned Jill to see if she could arrange a quick meeting in the main training room for all managers and supervisors. By the time he arrived, all the company leaders had made their way to the training room. When Lonnie had their full attention, he voiced a brief prayer and then gently shared the details of the morning.

As he concluded his remarks, Lonnie could not help but feel as though a giant vacuum had sucked every molecule of air from the room. As reality began to set in, some questions were raised about how to share the news with their employees. Lonnie gave some advice on how to handle the delivery of the information, and then let them know he and another chaplain would be making their way around the plant to care for employees who may be struggling emotionally.

"CONVERSION"

Lonnie asked the senior executive team to stay behind for a quick question. Once everyone else had left the room, he asked permission to hold a memorial service for Barbara at the company. He had mentioned it to Mr. Jones, who thought it was a good idea and said he would be honored to attend. Lonnie had received special training for holding such a service, but had no idea he would have to put it to use so soon. Chris had told Lonnie in training that many employees are reluctant to go to a funeral for various reasons but still need to grieve. They are often willing to attend a service held at the company that will honor their fallen friend.

Given that it was already afternoon on Monday, the service was set for 3:00 pm on Wednesday. This would allow for employees to attend from both the first and second shifts. Even though he had his hands full caring for grieving employees, Lonnie managed to assemble a group to help with the service. Jill put together a team to help transform the company's large cafeteria area into a respectful place to hold the service. Ellen in accounting took responsibility for the flowers. A group of men from the warehouse, who sang in a gospel choir at their church, volunteered to sing a couple of songs they knew to be Barbara's favorites. As the day wore on into evening, Lonnie prayed for God's blessing on the service, that it would honor Barbara's joyful life and also help the grieving employees to say goodbye to their dear friend.

Around 2:30 on Wednesday afternoon, Lonnie looked in the cafeteria and could hardly believe his eyes. It had been transformed into a beautiful sanctuary. The tables had been taken away, and chairs had been set up to make room for everyone who might attend. Mr. Jones walked in behind Lonnie, along with several of Barbara's aunts, uncles, and cousins. They had all been together earlier in the day for the church service held to honor Barbara's life. The turnout had been tremendous for the funeral and grave side service, followed by a wonderful luncheon at the church. Lonnie had been invited to sit on the platform with Reverend Pollard and to offer a prayer during the service. Reverend Pollard in turn graciously accepted Lonnie's invitation to join him at the memorial service at the plant. He would offer the prayer before Lonnie delivered a brief message to the employees who were now starting to assemble in the cafeteria.

Music began to play softly, and the room soon filled to capacity. The men's choir sang two beautiful songs, followed by David Reynolds' delivery of a touching eulogy. Reverend Pollard offered a deeply inspiring prayer for the friends and family, and then Lonnie stood to deliver a very brief, yet powerful message from the Bible. After sharing some wonderful words about the life of Barbara Jones, he said something that brought every ear in the cafeteria to full attention. "I know exactly what Barbara Jones would want me to tell you today." The silence in the room was almost deafening. He continued, "Our dear friend Barbara would want me to tell all of you, her nearest and dearest friends, how

"I know exactly what Barbara Jones would want me to tell you today."

to get to heaven so she will be able to visit with you again some day." With that he began to quickly tell them about the Jesus Barbara knew and loved and how they could know Him, too. He told them how Jesus had died for them just like He had for her and how He was simply waiting for them to turn from the broken ways of this world and fall into His loving arms, into a place of peace and rest.

A few moments later, Lonnie asked that they bow their heads while he prayed before they would be dismissed. Once he could tell every head was bowed and no one was looking around, he invited anyone who wanted to enter into a real and abiding lifetime relationship with Jesus to look up at him and follow him in a simple prayer that would change the course of their lives. Almost two dozen people immediately looked up at Lonnie, many with tears streaming down their faces. One of the tearful faces on the very back row was that of Johnny Clement. It was the first time Lonnie had ever seen him smile. What a sight, Johnny the antagonist smiling through tears. Lonnie knew they were tears of joy, peace, repentance, and relief.

Though he too was now crying, Lonnie asked the group to follow him in this simple prayer. "Dear Lord Jesus, I acknowledge before You that I have sinned in my life and need Your forgiveness. I believe that You died for my sins and rose from the grave. I want to turn from my sins, and I invite You to come into my heart and life and save me. I want to trust and follow you as my Lord and Savior. In Jesus' Name. Amen." After the prayer, Lonnie asked that they visit with him after the service was over, so he could give them a Bible to represent the significance of what had happened in their lives that day.

As the weeks and months passed following the service for Barbara Jones that late summer day, Lonnie often looked back in awe at how God could be glorified and lives could be eternally changed in a simple workplace cafeteria, regardless of how tragic the circumstances.

Leadership Transformers from Chapter Seven

🦋 **People grow together.** Strong peer alliances help a leader to grow. They also provide accountability and camaraderie that are not generally available in the regular daily routine.

🦋 **Recognize people regularly.** The tenure and accomplishments of staff are significant. Make time and take time to celebrate.

🦋 **People experience stress.** Recognize that employees are stressed and need decompression as much as you do.

🦋 **Provide practical help.** When your organization loses an employee through death, do everything possible to offer assistance to the employee's family and to your grieving associates.

🦋 **Prepare contingency plans.** Develop a process strategy for responding properly in the event of an employee fatality.

🦋 **Leaders demonstrate strength.** Workers look to leaders for comfort and strength in times of crisis.

🦋 **God changes hearts.** God can turn your workplace adversaries into your best advocates.

Leader's Ultimate Transformer Take Away

Anyone can pretend to be a leader when seas are calm and skies are clear. Only when the storms of life rage heavy does the true cream of leadership rise to the top.

C-Changer's Transforming Thought

"I used to ask God to help me. Then I asked if I might help Him. I ended up asking Him to do His work through me."

— *Hudson Taylor, 19th century missionary to China*

Caregiving Transformers from Chapter Seven

🦋 **Get with peers.** One of the best sources of support and fellowship for the workplace caregiver is relationships with other workplace caregivers.

🦋 **Always be ready.** Tragedy can occur in an instant.

🦋 **Provide helpful answers.** When calamity strikes an employee at work, be aware that other employees will want to have answers and will look to you for support and the truth.

🦋 **Kindly step aside.** When a family is served in a crisis by their pastor, always subordinate to the pastor and offer to help in any way they deem necessary.

🦋 **Honor the friend.** When there has been an employee death, seek permission from the company leadership to perform a brief, yet honoring, memorial service at the business location to help employees cope with grief.

🦋 **Let employees help.** Enlist other employees to participate in the brief memorial service and invite the family who has lost a loved one.

🦋 **Share the Good News.** Whenever possible, yet always with family permission, share the Good News of Jesus Christ with the mourners at a memorial service.

Caregiver's Ultimate Transformer Take Away

Grieving people need hope to survive. Never miss an opportunity to share the Good News of Jesus Christ with folks who are hurting.

Transformed by the Word

"What this means is that those who become Christians become new persons. They are not the same anymore, for the old life is gone. A new life has begun."
– 2 Corinthians 5:17 (NLT)

Conclusion

My prayer is that this book has allowed you to see your workplace in a totally new light. I pray that you will see it as one of the greatest mission fields on Earth, a place where God can use you as a transforming agent in the lives of people you see every day.

Let's review the realities of the "7 C's":

Christ: Jesus is the central power at work in the marketplace. He is the glue that holds everything together. He is the cornerstone of all the "C's". Make Him the central part of your workplace ministry and you can not fail.

Call: As believers we are all called to be workplace ministry transformers, agents of change in a fallen world. Accept God's call on your life and start the process today.

Confidentiality: Your level of influence in the lives of people in your mission field will be in direct proportion to your ability to bridle your tongue. As you practice developing your skill as a "strategic listener", you will see your ministry explode.

Compassion: If you want to have true compassion for people in your mission field, emulate Jesus and the way He dealt with people in the marketplace. Regardless of their circumstances, He loved and had mercy on them.

CONCLUSION

Control: Never forget, God is in control and we are not. Nothing you will encounter will catch Him off guard, and He will make sure you have every resource necessary to accomplish His will.

Consistency: People crave consistency in the lives of their leaders. Every area of your life will be enhanced as you systematically embed consistency into your leadership lifestyle.

Conversion: This is where everything comes together from an eternal perspective. Look at it as your true retirement account. This is like literally laying up treasures in Heaven. God has been at work in the hearts of people with whom you work for a long time. All you have to do is be available with the Good News and allow God to take it from there.

I encourage you to start now in prayer, by asking God to anoint and empower you as a workplace ministry leader. Then let us know how things are going in your work by visiting us on the web at: www.lanphierpress.com. My prayer is that God will richly bless every effort you make for Him in our great mission field.

To talk with someone about having a chaplain for your company, please call: 800-825-0310 ext. 208.

❦ Other books by Mark Cress

The Third Awakening

Prepare yourself for a fun and fast paced story about how God uses events in the lives of ordinary people to change the course of history for millions. After reading this book, you may never look at yourself, your friends, or the world around you the same way again. Also available in Spanish and as an Audio book.

Twenty Words That Will Change Your Life Forever

In *Twenty Words That Will Change Your Life Forever*, you will discover 10 "core values" that can help in every situation that you face as you go through each day. When deeply integrated into all areas of your life, from the routine to the unexpected, these "core values" can help you make genuine changes that will last for eternity.

The Complete Corporate Chaplain's Handbook

In recent years, many books have been written about the rise of spirituality in the workplace. While this trend is important to understand, there has been, to date, no "how to" guide for the corporate chaplain. This text exists to fill the procedural and information gap for workplace ministry. Keep this book on hand as a reference for the many opportunities of ministry in the greatest mission field on earth: the workplace.

These titles are available through Lanphier Press.
www.lanphierpress.com